# THE 2012 ELECTION
# AND
# BEYOND

# THE 2012 ELECTION AND BEYOND

Why the Selfish Coalition of the Superrich, the Fundamentalists, and the Closed-Minded Should Be Defeated

## GIESERIL

iUniverse, Inc.
Bloomington

**The 2012 Election and Beyond**
**Why the Selfish Coalition of the Superrich, the Fundamentalists,**
**and the Closed-Minded Should Be Defeated**

*iUniverse books may be ordered through booksellers or by contacting:*

*iUniverse*
*1663 Liberty Drive*
*Bloomington, IN 47403*
*www.iuniverse.com*
*1-800-Authors (1-800-288-4677)*

*ISBN: 978-1-4759-3637-7 (sc)*
*ISBN: 978-1-4759-3638-4 (e)*
*ISBN: 978-1-4759-3639-1 (dj)*

*Library of Congress Control Number: 2012912196*

*Printed in the United States of America*

*iUniverse rev. date: 07/10/2012*

# CONTENTS

## Epigram

There are things to be said
And said again—
Even if we have heard
Them before.
And so,
With apologies:
To all those who care,
For all of us.

Gieseril

I completed writing this book in May of 2012. In the coming months before the 2012 elections, unforeseen events could make some of my statements and emphasis on certain issues more or less important or relevant than others. However, I believe, the core issues discussed in this book and opinions expressed will remain highly relevant for a long time to come – way beyond the 2012 elections

# INTRODUCTION
# MORE THAN JUST THE ECONOMY

It has been said repeatedly in the recent past that the 2012 US election is all about the economy. Though it is arguably correct that the economy is the main issue in the coming election, an equally important (or more important) issue also needs to be addressed. Are we totally selfish and unconcerned about those who have less or are different from us in terms of beliefs, or are we less selfish and more concerned about the plight of those who have less or maintain different belief systems or life philosophies?

There are two sides arrayed against each other in this election. On one side is the coalition of selfishness made up of and spearheaded by the wealth and money of the superrich (which provides the impetus for selfishness). That side consists of fundamentalists and closed-minded individuals. On the other side, there are those who are less selfish, more open-minded, and more inclined to have concern for others—especially those who have less.

This book is about why people should vote against the selfish coalition of the superrich, the fundamentalists, and the closed-minded people to avoid catastrophe for the ordinary folks—the poor and open-minded people of our country.

In 2008, a majority of the people voted to elect Barack Obama as president and to maintain a Democrat majority in Congress and the Senate. When this election took place, our country was in the worst predicament (economically) that it had been in since the Great Depression. Eight years of rule by the coalition of selfishness had left the country in ruins. There was a devastating recession; unemployment was high and skyrocketing. We were mired in two wars that were, at the very least, started for vague and controversial reasons.

During the past three years, the country has struggled through difficult times as a result of what was inherited from the previous administration. Some good things have happened during these years. Perhaps the greatest accomplishment of the present administration is the enactment of the law to provide health insurance for almost all people in the country (which is to be implemented, step-by-step, in the coming years unless the Supreme Court makes it difficult). The coalition of selfishness, including their presidential candidates, has promised to repeal this law if they come into power, leaving millions of Americans without any chance to obtain affordable health insurance.

Another accomplishment of the present administration has been the winding down of the wars in Iraq and Afghanistan. These wars have been causing unnecessary death and injury to our young people. Plus, war drains the country of money that could be used for the needs of its citizens—especially those who have been badly hurt by the recession (caused by the policies of the previous administration).

Now the coalition of selfishness and their candidates want us to forget all that happened before 2008, including the recession. The recession started prior to the 2008 election and was a direct result of the actions taken by the coalition of selfishness. It resulted, in part, from the previous administration enabling the superrich and the greedy to run amok with their unregulated financial activity, which ruined our economy and the housing market. This includes the tax cuts for the superrich (remember: there's a superrich presidential candidate who pays a lower tax rate than most of us), leaving very little to spend on the necessities of the country.

What we face in the 2012 election, in simple terms, is a struggle between ordinary open-minded people and the coalition led by the superrich with a closed-minded set of followers. This latter group rejects open-mindedness regarding what scientific advances teach us and what history teaches us about the need for tolerance and the need to reevaluate our beliefs. These ideas become more relevant as we humans continue to understand more and more about our life on earth, our planet, and the universe itself. This closed-minded group does not want us to evaluate for ourselves the beliefs that have been thrust upon humanity through millennia and books compiled thousands of years back. They insist those sources contain all truth for all time to come. They want us to blindly obey such beliefs, which are often irrational. The beliefs also cause animosity toward those who believe in other systems, ideas, or philosophies (including open-minded and rational people). This, in short, is a summary of the choice we have to make in this election. Will we vote for the concerns of the majority of people in this country, or will we side with the selfish coalition of the superrich, the fundamentalists, and the closed-minded. The selfish coalition provides unlimited financial support for their group because they, the superrich, believe that the coalition will protect their financial interests. They also believe the coalition will keep the middle class and the poor in line, which is an ideal situation for them, because those people are seen as a threat to unlimited greed.

If we do not vote against the coalition of selfishness, or if we do not vote at all in the coming election, there will be terrible consequences. Many ordinary folks (and many of the poor) often fail to vote because they think their votes do not matter, the rich and the powerful will always control their lives no matter what, or they are not informed enough to make a good decision. But, if these would-be voters fail, the selfish coalition of the superrich, the fundamentalists, and the closed-minded will take control of our lives once more and repeat the catastrophe they unleashed before 2008. This time around, it may be even worse—they have promised to undo all the progress that has occurred since the current administration came into power. For starters, they have promised to repeal the health care law that the present administration enacted. This means that roughly fifty million ordinary Americans who have no health insurance and cannot take care of their medical needs will be in danger. That is what the coalition of selfishness will do, and that is just for starters.

# CHAPTER I
## SELFISHNESS VERSUS UNSELFISHNESS

There are reasons how and why a selfish coalition of the superrich, the fundamentalists, and the closed-minded came about. People who are superrich (and in general, those who consider amassing huge amounts of money and wealth to be the primary or only goal on this earth) are usually programmed to pursue an education and work life aimed at amassing wealth at any cost. This hoarding, shields them from being concerned about the serious problems of mankind—especially the problems of those who do not have much. For the superrich, it is all about money—and more and more of it for themselves. It does not matter to them how their money-making actions affect others. It is not their problem. In fact, they justify their behavior by rationalizing that it is how business works. (Anyone remember the infamous quip, "Don't they know how business works?") One gets ahead by putting others out of business. It is their philosophy. They would even claim that this country is built on that principle—it was the wish of our founding fathers. That is the American way, they say.

They give little importance to the well-being of all citizens, including the middle class and the poor. Their singular aim is to make as much money for themselves as possible. They seek to hold on to that money and make more and more for themselves before handing it over (with the accompanying philosophy) to their descendants. In this way, they hope to perpetuate a family dynasty committed to their philosophy. Anything else they do is essentially related to this ideology, which is the central theme of their lives. Unfortunately for them, in a democracy they cannot accomplish their goals on their own. They are a small minority—the 1 percent, if you will. They need to form a coalition that will support their philosophy, and they find two groups that will help them accomplish their goals. One group is brainwashed into believing fundamentalist philosophies originating thousands of years back (when there were no scientific facts to support a rational view of the world). What one has to come to terms with as a result of a rational or scientific inquiry about man's predicament may be painful to accept. But facts are facts, and painful as they may be, we shouldn't embrace fantasy instead of them.

Our forefathers also looked for comfort in supernatural and religious beliefs. But it is better to accept scientific facts and try to improve our lot in this world than force ourselves to believe in some fundamentalist ideology that leads to terrorizing others.

Unfortunately, the fundamentalists refuse to accept scientific facts, and they are determined to maintain their irrational thinking and force it upon others by influencing policy. Related to this group are those who have a very narrow approach to anything new, especially anything that is scientific and rational. They may not be exactly fundamentalists in their religious beliefs, but being closed-minded makes them very similar to the fundamentalists in terms of how they approach issues. They reject new understandings, especially any knowledge that comes through progress in science, scientific ways of thinking, or what could be learned from history.

The superrich use these two groups to create a voting bloc, and they support them with money. They use the two groups to accomplish their goals (based on the selfish principle of amassing more and more wealth). They ignore all else, particularly the plight of those who have much less—in spite of their hard work—such as those without jobs and the poor. It is not that the superrich have any particular philosophical or religious affinity with the fundamentalist group—after all, greed and apathy toward the poor goes against most religious tenets. They associate themselves with such closed-minded groups for one purpose only: to gain political power and protect their interest in making excessive amounts of money at the expense of others.

I call this coalition of the superrich, the fundamentalists, and the closed-minded the coalition of selfishness because they make life all about themselves. They desire to make excessive amounts of money at the expense of others and to thrust their fundamentalist and closed-minded ideology on others at any cost (including bringing the government to a standstill if they can't get their way). It is their way or no way. They reject compromise, which is essential for democracy.

The question before us in the coming election and beyond is this: Are we going to be a nation of selfish people who are concerned only about our own welfare, or are we going to be a nation of people who are also concerned about the welfare of those less fortunate than many of us? (By less fortunate, I mean less fortunate in circumstances of birth, wealth, ability, genetic endowment, innate intelligence, physical health and predisposition to illnesses of body and mind which ruin a person's chance to have a reasonable life, and less fortunate in the circumstances that make it difficult to get integrated into the main stream of society - whether it be issues of skin color, ethnicity, sexual orientation with which we are born, or in the unlucky turn of events that may come our way in life, over which we may have little control.

More than anything else, this issue—whether we are going to be a selfish people or a people concerned about the welfare of those less fortunate than we are—may be the key factor that distinguishes and defines the opposite sides arrayed in this election. We already know what the selfish coalition would be for. We know the selfish coalition sees the less fortunate as inconsequential or a threat to society. They explain away all problems of the less fortunate by calling them willfully lazy or irresponsible.

This issue of selfishness versus concern for the less fortunate may be the most infrequently mentioned theme in the present election for various reasons, but it may nevertheless underlie all the topics that are being hotly contested in this election. For example, how should we aid our ailing economy? Which and how *much* resources should we allocate for what? Which tax and spending cuts should we make, should we maintain the opportunity for all of us including the presently uninsured, to obtain health insurance or whether we will repeal the law that provides such opportunity, because many of us already have insurance and we are selfish and don't want to jeopardize what we have, by providing coverage for those who have none, or even consider the plight of the uninsured not a concern for us, as it is their problem only. Also think about these questions: Should we spend money on education or give tax cuts to the superrich (leaving nothing to spend on programs that are vital to society)? Should we claim that our belief system is better than someone else's? All of these questions will be directly or indirectly related to this central theme: Are we going to be a nation of selfish people, or are we going to be a group of people also concerned about the well-being of those who are less fortunate than we are?

Whether the coalition of selfishness couches their arguments in terms of keeping government out of all aspects of our lives or in terms of safeguarding our liberty, the issue is the same: Are we going to be a selfish (*me, me, and only me*) nation, or will we have concern in our hearts for those who are less fortunate than we are?

So now we have the two opposing groups arrayed in the battle of the 2012 election. Let us be very aware of the choices: The coalition of selfishness led by the superrich and accompanied by the fundamentalists and closed-minded are on one side. On the other side are those who are less selfish, those who have an open mind, and those who are concerned about the less fortunate. This is our choice in the 2012 election.

This is the ideological battle of the 2012 election and beyond, and yes, it is about more than the economy.

In this ideological battle for justice and fairness for all, our votes will matter—a great deal indeed!

Vote!

# CHAPTER II
# THE ECONOMY

During the past several years, from the time of the previous administration, which represented the coalition of the selfish and landed the country in the horrendous recession we went through because of their selfishness oriented philosophy, which states that, if the government makes it possible for the wealthy to become more and more wealthy, everything will be fine with the country. Essentially, the coalition under discussion here, the one consumed by selfishness, believes in that same philosophy and wants to take us back to the catastrophic policies of the previous, failed administration. But they want the conditions for the ordinary people and the poor to be even worse, by favoring the superrich and the privileged even more than the previous administration did. According to this philosophy, the more prosperous the rich are, their attempts to make more and more money will result in more jobs and opportunities for ordinary people and the poor (and thus the whole country will be just fine (think *"trickle down"*).

However, what happened as a result of that ideology (when it was tried the last time by the previous, failed administration) was a disaster, from which we are still reeling. Such a philosophy, combined with other reckless actions favoring the high and mighty, made the economy weaker and weaker until the economy of the whole country crumbled. That philosophy ushered in the "great recession," from which we are only just beginning to recover. With their policies giving the superrich everything they asked for and more and the loosening of regulations that allowed the high and mighty to play as they pleased, the economy crumbled, the housing market was ruined, and unemployment shot up. Households were left impoverished and people lost their houses, savings, and pensions. Young and middle-aged people—even the very educated—could not find work, could not support themselves, and could not get health insurance. By the time of the 2008 election, the country had collapsed. The country was in a terrible condition, the likes of which we have never witnessed in several generations.

Fortunately, the coalition of the superrich, the fundamentalists, and the closed-minded lost the 2008 election and the country got a breather—a second chance.

The damage done to the economy by the philosophy of selfishness was so bad that an avalanche of ill effects was unleashed. The coalition's reckless actions made recovery from the economic disaster extremely difficult and slow, in spite of several programs instituted by the present administration to help the recovery. Fortunately, we started seeing some signs of recovery from the severe recession, in early 2012, though the problems of other regions of the world, especially Europe are hindering our recovery at the time of this writing. Overall there has been resurgence of hope for ordinary people and the need for a government concerned about their well being and with an urgency of purpose on their behalf is more essential than ever before. This is no time for "trickle down."

Our work remains incomplete, and we can't let the philosophy of selfishness drag us back into the ditch they left us in before the 2008 election. Of course, the coalition of selfishness wants to misguide us by touting the same philosophy that ruined us—as if it were a panacea for all of the country's problems. They champion this philosophy even though it is the same one that almost destroyed the country and made America the laughingstock of the world by 2008. They do not want us to remember what was happening before 2008 (and that it is their failed philosophy that caused ruin and destroyed us). Now they want a rerun of it, except they want it to be a worse "hunger game" this time around.

Due to the propaganda of the coalition of selfishness, many of us misunderstood the slow recovery from the last economic recession as the result of the ineffectiveness of the present administration. Many of us fell victim to the propaganda unleashed by the coalition of selfishness.

Since the 2010 interim congressional elections, when the coalition of selfishness took over Congress, they have opposed practically every positive suggestion put forth by the present administration and the progressive majority in the Senate. This has produced a stalemate. Their aim is to keep the economy weak and joblessness high so that they can blame the present administration for that situation. That would allow them to get back into power by winning the 2012 election, capturing the presidency, and gaining a majority in both the Congress and the Senate. In this way, they could reinstate the rule that brought ordinary people misery. This time they want it to be harsher for ordinary people and the poor. The coalition wants to cut whatever the ordinary people have gained through generations of effort and struggles. They want to repeal the health care law that gives the uninsured a chance to have insurance for the first time in the history of this country. In my mind, the health care law is the single most important achievement of the present administration.

They brag about denying health insurance for those who do not have it, as if that were a great feat to accomplish. Taking away the right of the uninsured to have insurance, they claim, would be one of their greatest achievements. They take pride in having a harsh philosophy that does not concern itself with those who have less. As long as they protect the rich and privileged from paying their fair share in taxes and keeping their perks, they are happy.

Their economic agenda, in brief, involves an ideology, laws, and regulations that favor the rich and the selfish and cut benefits for everyone else. They have no interest in fairness.

The coalition of selfishness wants to brainwash us with their propaganda that government should not be involved in economic matters, except to make it easy for private corporations to make greater profits. They also say we should leave everything but the defense of the country to be run by for-profit, private companies. The only role they see for the government in economic matters is to loosen all regulations that were created to protect the average person from exploitation by those who are consumed by greed.

The selfish coalition wants government to make it possible for individuals and corporations to pursue profits with no limitations or rules (and with little concern for what happens to others in the process). They want a slash-and-burn philosophy to rule, whereby anything goes in the pursuit of wealth. They have little concern for what happens to others in the process, what happens to the workers, whose toil—more often than not—allows them to amass their wealth. They would like to claim that all wealth is created by their genius in financial matters. They interpret the phrase *pursuit of happiness* to mean *pursuit of money at any cost and without consideration for anyone else.* Hence, they feel that government should stay out of their way and let them run amok. In order to achieve this, they want to take over the presidency, the Congress, and the Senate. In this way, their ruthless philosophy could once more rule the country and allow more cash to flow into *their* pockets. The poor will be left with less and less. It is fine, they say. It is what this country is supposed to be all about, according to them.

We beg to differ. We don't mind a country that gives plenty of opportunity for those who think making money is the most important reason for human beings to be on this planet. We don't mind them keeping a fair share of that money. But we also want it to be a country that gives the ordinary person and the poor person a chance to improve his or her life situation without having to depend on the kindness of the superrich. That sort of dependence, our recent history has shown, will never work. The members of the coalition of selfishness (led by the superrich) are only concerned about themselves and their own philosophy. They believe nobody is responsible for others—no matter how weak or unfortunate that other person may be. They assume everyone is born into this world with equal ability and in equal circumstances and if someone can't make it, it is his or her fault. They don't mind that unfortunate people suffer and even die without health care. (Remember the applause in their debates!)

Any improvement in the plight of ordinary people and the poor, they want us to believe, should not be a concern of the government. They want us to believe that, once the wealthy become wealthier, with cutthroat tactics and minimal regulations, they will have so much left over that the ordinary and the poor will automatically get a bit of it. Thus, everything would be fine, they say. "Government, just stay out of the way and all will be as it is destined to be," is their mantra.

They want government power, however, to make government go away while they collect their government handouts and perks, so that their coalition of selfishness led by the super-rich can do as they please without any controls. Once they attain governmental power, they will get all the perks they don't want others to have. They will work perpetually to make government go away, while collecting government checks for themselves, to help them and their supporters pursue money and thrust their fundamentalist and closed-minded philosophy on all aspects of life in the country. They want this state of affairs to continue with each election cycle. They're trying to fool us with their failed philosophy, once again. Let us not fall for it.

Lincoln famously said, "Government of the people, by the people, for the people shall not perish from the earth." And that sentiment will remain a fact as long as mankind exists. Humans will always strive to establish and maintain such a concerned government. Without such a government, our plight will be the plight of people in totalitarian and repressive regimes elsewhere.

To safeguard the nation's economy that will do justice for all, we need to become aware of the issues involved in this 2012 election. Once we are more informed, we will not be fooled by the illogical brainwashing the selfish coalition is unleashing on us—especially their desire for us to forget what went on before 2008. We can't forget about the horrendous recession their failed philosophy and attitude left us with. That awareness and clear thinking will help us see the issues at stake in this election and prepare us to avoid potential ruin.

Vote!

# CHAPTER III
# THE HIGH UNEMPLOYMENT RATE AND THE MILLIONS OF AMERICANS WHO CANNOT FIND GAINFUL EMPLOYMENT

Though, due to no fault of their own, millions of Americans have not been able to find gainful employment during the last several years. This is a direct result of the horrendous recession and the subsequent loss of employment the previous administration gave us as a parting gift. Though there has been gradual improvement in this situation—in spite of obstructions by the coalition of selfishness in the Congress, which blocked every move to improve the plight of the unemployed—more needs to be done. When the selfish coalition took over in 2000, it implemented trickle-down economic policies, which favor the rich. The coalition gave the rich the opportunity to grab anything they could get by establishing a loose regulatory system.

If the coalition of selfishness (led by the superrich) wins in 2012, that unfair system will be thrust upon us again—and they make no bones about it. They do not want us to think that it is a failed policy that seriously hurt the ordinary people. Instead, they want us to believe that the problem of high unemployment started with the present administration. They want us to forget that they are the ones who set in motion the spike in unemployment to near depression level and kept it high. They want us to forget that the present high unemployment situation came from the calamitous downward spiral set in motion by their own previous administration. They want us to forget that it was the present administration that managed to reverse the course.

With the efforts in the past three years—implemented by the present administration—we have been seeing signs of hope. There has been improvement in the job market, though the situation is still tragic for millions of people. This grim reality is especially true for the unemployed young—they were unlucky enough to be dumped into a poor job market without even basic medical insurance. Almost every developed country provides health insurance for its citizens as a birthright. But we Americans are denied this right. Continuous effort by a government for the people, by the people, and of the people will be required to improve this situation. Let us not bring in a selfish government to ruin everything for us once again. Let us not worsen the plight of the unemployed and the young people coming out of our educational institutions.

The coalition of the selfish (which wants to continuously fool us with falsehoods) wants us to remember only that the unemployment rate is still high. It does not want us to use our thinking and memory to figure out that the horrendous worsening in the job market and economy came about on their watch (due to mismanagement). The present, hopeful situation and positive trajectory (in terms of job opportunities) are significant improvements from the disaster we were left with. If the present administration is voted back to continue its thoughtful and concerted effort to help the ordinary people, opportunities for jobs in this country will continue to improve.

Bringing the coalition of selfishness back to power will be a disaster for the employment situation in the country. The idea that the government should stay back and "let the markets work" (that the free enterprise system will solve all problems) is misguided. The unemployed are not collateral damage in a war between private enterprises to decide victors and losers. Those ideas will destroy the hopes of the unemployed. The youngsters coming out of our educational institutions after years of earnest effort must not find that their society, their elders, and their government have betrayed them.

Americans were lulled into believing that they could study anything they wanted and find plenty of jobs waiting, no matter what. They were told that getting a foot into an all-about-money firm and manipulating papers and accounts could give them a luxurious lifestyle. Those ideas have been put to a stress test in the recent past and found to be foolish. During the past two decades—when many other countries were preparing their youngsters for jobs the world wants done (and for which a combination of natural gifts and hard work were necessary)—we were lulled into believing anything would do. Now we are waking up to the reality that we have fallen behind in terms of science and technology—the fields that are propelling advances in the world and where a lot of good jobs are.

We have depended too much on expensive and unaffordable private institutions to provide our youngsters with the skills they need to succeed in today's world. Often what is bestowed is a veneer of superiority and privilege, a cutthroat mentality, and a tuition debt that lasts a lifetime. Slashing government support for public institutions and universities (where most of our youngsters could receive an affordable education and develop job skills) is not helping the unemployed or the competitiveness of this country. There is a frenzy to cut all government programs and aid. The selfish coalition has been demanding such cuts, and they use them to hold the government hostage. They use cuts as a bargaining chip to protect the low 15 percent tax rate of the superrich. With such cuts in spending for education, how can public institutions provide the education and skills necessary for the vast majority of our youngsters? Above all, who is there to spearhead the philosophy that the education of our children (preparing them for the jobs of today and tomorrow) is a national priority? Who is spearheading the philosophy that we should treat our children as our national wealth and their education as our national cause? There is no successful nation of tomorrow unless our children succeed. Today, there is great doubt in terms of what the coming decades will bring for our youngsters (and, subsequently, our nation).

We need a government willing to take a leadership role in preparing our children for the jobs of today and the innovations of tomorrow. We do not want a government preoccupied with cutting all services and aid, to safeguard the unjust 15 percent tax rate of millionaires and billionaires.

The superrich have hijacked the coalition of selfishness to protect their greed and ill-begotten tax breaks. They have no interest in spending government money for the average youngster's education and skill building. They see their tax breaks as the highest priority, and they have deluded the rest of the selfish coalition into thinking that a person's responsibility is only to himself or herself. The ideas of the selfish coalition (couched in a libertarian veneer), proclaims that a person should look after himself or herself and be free to enjoy liberty as they define it and what happens to others should not be their concern. The selfish coalition tells us we should just enjoy our freedom—even if that means the less fortunate of us perish. The people in the coalition rationalize that there are already people and organizations practicing charity to help the needy. They say that if those folks have nothing better to do, let them spend time and money on the unfortunate people ... the world will go on fine. Government should just stay out of all affairs, and everything will be fine, according to them. Let the unlucky and infirm die, if need be, as long as others have liberty. (Remember their debates and applause. I am glad some of those guys are not practicing doctors anymore!)

Unfortunately, things will not be fine if the government stays out of the proper education and skill building of our youngsters. We want a government that is willing to take a leadership role in conjunction with the best minds and universities in the country. This will allow great thinkers to put forth ideas that will revolutionize our educational system and prepare our children to be good citizens. Our children will also have the knowledge and skills necessary to compete with anyone in today's global job market. We have to put our money where our mouth is. To accomplish this, we need to ask everyone to pay reasonable taxes. Our children's future is more important than safeguarding the ill-begotten 15 percent tax rate of the superrich. The superrich have no legitimate use for that money anyway, and they end up establishing Super PACs and such to subvert democracy. They have an obscene amount of money lying around that it corrupts their minds even more.

Vote! Vote against the coalition of selfishness to prevent it from destroying the lives of the unemployed and the future of our children.

# CHAPTER IV
# TAX

The coalition of selfishness wants to continue giving unjustified tax cuts to the very wealthy, even if it leaves the country without adequate money and resources for tasks essential for the well-being of the country. These tasks include needed improvement to our decaying infrastructure, such as building and repairing roads and bridges and modernizing our transportation system. They also include aid for education, which is vital for helping our children grow up to be capable and responsible adults. Also, they consist of the programs that provide health insurance and financial help for the poor who can't fend for themselves, the mentally ill, and the physically disabled. And there are many other areas where government help is needed beyond these areas of pressing needs.

Whether we like it or not all societies will have to provide assistance for the very poor, the mentally ill, and the physically disabled. Otherwise, they will not be real societies worth their names at all.

People who repeat the mantra, "Cut, cut, cut"—including the politicians who repeat that mantra to gain the votes of the closed-minded and prejudiced—do not seem to understand that civilized society could not exist without providing such services. Without them, we would be like countries that have no infrastructure, no worthwhile and affordable educational institutions, and no proper system for caring for the mentally ill and the infirm.

Either the coalition's politicians are not open to reality, or they want to delude themselves and brainwash us into believing that undue tax cuts for the superrich is fine— as if leaving no money in the government's coffers were acceptable and the country could proceed on its merry way. One argument they come up with is that there are innumerable programs and services that can be cut without any harm. It is true that there are ways to streamline and make programs more efficient in most instances. But beyond a point, cutting more and more won't make any sense. The level of deterioration in services and the level of suffering in the country will go up so high that it won't be the United States anymore.

Take, for example, Social Security. For a good majority of elderly people in the country, Social Security is the only source of income. Most people who have to live entirely on Social Security retirement benefits lead a difficult life. They just scrape by (at best) on an income for which they worked long years and contributed from every pay check of theirs, often in low-paying and difficult jobs. Yet one of the first things the "cut only" group talks about is interfering with the Social Security system (though the group camouflages this with ambiguous terms and rationalizations).

One look at countries where there is no government-run Social Security system and one is appalled at the plight of the elderly, the mentally ill, and the physically disabled. Even the most cold-hearted will agree that is no way for the United States to treat its citizens. If one looks at the financial situation of the elderly who live on Social Security alone, one will have no doubt that there is nothing there to cut. It is also important to keep reminding ourselves that Social Security benefits are not gifts—they are not charity. Social Security is what a worker has earned through hard work and years of toil. It is what the country owes as part of the contract the country makes with every working American. Without meeting its obligations (regarding the Social Security contract), America won't be America anymore. The coalition of selfishness wants us to purchase individual contracts with greedy private financial companies (the same way they ask us to shop for health insurance on our own with companies that want to make money on our death beds, the plan they have for us after repealing the present health care law). Good luck!

Such lack of money and resources in the government's hands will also affect Medicaid and Medicare. Millions upon millions of the retired elderly, the poor, and the disabled (both mentally and physically) rely upon such aid. People need Medicaid and Medicare to maintain a reasonably healthy life and minimum comforts in old age. After all, advancing age and diseases ravage the body and mind of almost all people before their end comes.

A country exists on income it derives from its natural resources and taxes it collects from its citizens. In turn, it provides protection and services, only a government can provide effectively. Historically, our country (like many others) has provided certain services to its citizens. As decades and centuries go by, especially in this era of computers and automation, there will be services that the private sector can provide equally well—or even more efficiently. This is something the citizens and government have to come to terms with. A government that is responsive to its citizens—as a government by and for the people will be—can and should make such determinations at appropriate times.

To claim the superrich should have their 15 percent tax rate so they can enjoy more of their income than ordinary people, does not make sense. The argument that the income that the government loses by such an unfair tax system will not affect needed services, upkeep, and modernization of infrastructure, transportation, and other vital services does not make sense. It is an argument made to brainwash us into thinking that the government can live with much less money and there won't be any consequences. The warped rationale entails the for-profit, private sector picking up the slack by charging us for services. One is not sure how the for-profit sector will take care of those who can't pay because they are severely or chronically ill and disabled. One is not sure how the poor, many of whom have been dealt an unfair hand from day one, will survive in that system. How much the private companies will have to charge us for the roads, bridges, and highways they will take over. Imagine the tolls! If they are bad now, watch out when the for-profit companies take over. They won't be our roads and highways and bridges anymore. As for the superrich, their 15 percent tax rate will leave them plenty for the tolls—if they don't own the highways and bridges outright by that time.

We need a tax system that makes everyone pay a fair percentage of their income. We can't have a system in which the person who makes $50,000 per year pays a higher percentage in taxes than a millionaire or billionaire. The government does need the money a fair tax system will generate to provide just and vital services.

This is another reason to vote against the coalition of the selfish (led by the superrich). The coalition desperately wants to protect the unfair tax system, which was hoisted on us by the previous administration formed by the coalition. This tax system was one of the main reasons why we ended up in the calamitous recession.

Vote!

# Chapter V
# No Need for Government?

The coalition of the selfish has touted the idea that government should only be concerned with the defense of the country. The coalition states that all other activities should be left to individuals and private companies whose sole purpose is to make as much profit as possible.

If the coalition of selfishness is given control of our government, it would seek to cut down the role of government to almost nothing. The government's role, essentially, would be to manage the army for the defense of the country ... and very little else. But the government has many other functions today, such as making sure all children get a decent education and are prepared for the jobs of today and tomorrow, establishing fair access to healthcare for all, aiding the extremely poor and disabled, and creating rules by which private companies and banking institutions should operate. All of these are targets for the coalition if its members come into power. For-profit companies and for-profit people see only dollar signs in whatever they do. Unless these people and companies are regulated properly, they will ruin people's lives.

Yes, too much regulation can stifle growth, job creation, and even our quality of life. But too little regulation can cause more damage to people—as we saw during the latest recession. Poorly regulated Wall Street institutions, banks, and related financial institutions (with their illegitimate and reckless activities) wrecked our housing market, our job market, and our pension savings. These catastrophes ruined the lives of almost all of us. Any institution (or individual) that has excessive profit (and profit at any cost) as the primary motive can do damage to the average person ... unless its activities are properly regulated. A party or coalition that is primarily concerned with how much profit its supporters can make and has no concern or awareness for the social consequences of such actions can leave the ordinary person and the disabled in the ditch. Those who say they do not want the government to regulate anything also want to get government power. That way, they can give full reign to their supporters who are mostly in the (high) profit-making businesses or thrust their blind and extreme fundamentalist beliefs into the policy-making arenas.

These are some of the serious issues at stake in this election. And these are the reasons to make sure the coalition of the selfish does not come into power. Each vote matters. There is too much to lose for every one of us.

Vote!

# CHAPTER VI
## GOVERNMENT'S ROLE IN FINDING SOLUTIONS FOR THE MENTAL AND PHYSICAL ILLNESSES THAT AFFLICT US

Without government playing a leading role, the most serious of our mental and physical health problems may never be solved.

Private companies by themselves won't find cures for the most serious and prevalent illnesses that affect mankind. These include illnesses such as bipolar disorder, schizophrenia, AIDS (and other life-threatening viral illnesses), various cancers, autism spectrum disorders, Alzheimer's (and other dementias), parkinsonism, autoimmune diseases that cause havoc to our system, and various other illnesses that affect the brain and other organs and turns human existence into a meaningless misery, very often. Private companies will not pursue projects unless they feel they can make a profit in the near-term. Many of the illnesses that have baffled us and resisted our efforts to truly understand how they are caused and what exactly goes wrong require scientific explorations of a very basic, profound, and complex nature. Those explorations will require collaboration among scientific agencies, universities, research laboratories, and clinicians. Otherwise, it will be impossible to accomplish real progress quickly enough to give hope for the present and coming generations.

The idea that private companies by themselves will find solutions for the major health problems facing our country is false. Unless such companies feel that they can make enormous profits in a quick enough time period by pursuing a project, they won't bother. Profits usually result from developing and marketing a drug that can be prescribed for a very large number of people for a very long period of time (and thus make a huge profit for the company). And if a project doesn't fit that profile, these companies won't put money and effort into such measures. If they can make a huge profit by doing something comparatively simple and get it approved by the Food and Drug Administration one way or another, they will jump at that opportunity. This often entails satisfying the regulatory criteria and unleashing a huge marketing campaign to sell the drugs to millions of people and take their enormous profits.

These companies look for projects where they can tinker at the edges to keep the money-making machine going. It's an easier method than worrying about solving the health problems of humanity. Such fundamental solutions will require collaborative effort by large pools of very capable scientists and clinicians from multiple facilities. These facilities include research universities, hospitals and other clinical facilities, and centers such as the National Institute of Health. Collaboration among these organizations and from across the globe will lead to real progress. It will require large infusions of money and effort—decade after decade—with the hope that, eventually, we will find solutions to the devastating genetic and other illnesses that wreak havoc to individuals, our country, and the world itself. To find lasting and permanent solutions to such tragic illnesses causing misery today and even threatening the extinction of humanity, the government constituted by us— the government of, for, and by the people—has to take a leadership role. Without such an effort (devoid of the profit motive), the plight of humanity will not improve, and we will face a horrendous future.

No reasonable person would be against government agencies collaborating with private agencies, private universities (with their impressive research capacities), and even pharmaceutical and other companies to find solutions to these problems. But to think that private drug companies will take a well-motivated, leading role in unraveling the mysteries of these illnesses and find solutions to them is just wishful thinking. It is not realistic, and it would be foolish and irresponsible to leave the coming generations to fend for themselves. We must do our share and hand the baton to them to carry on the good work—generation after generation. The whole fate of humanity depends on such dedicated efforts without financial profits as the goal.

To think that companies whose motive is to make the biggest profit they can, in the shortest time possible and with the least expenditure, will give the highest priority for basic research to solve complex health problems that may be rooted in evolutionary biology from time immemorial, is illogical. But that basic research, aimed at finding the root causes of illnesses and syndromes (such as the ones mentioned before) is vital. In this context, anyone who has done considerable and well-meaning work to ameliorate the suffering of people affected by such illnesses must be shocked at how widespread some of these disorders are. There is a huge genetic component to many of these illnesses, especially bipolar disorder. Bipolar disorder is spreading like a wildfire throughout our country, both in adults and in children. It may even be the number one cause for human misery in our country in the near future ... if it is not already. Bipolar disorder, which is entirely a genetic illness threaten to destroy the very fabric of our society unless we find not only effective treatment but a permanent solution to it by unraveling its genetic underpinnings and find methods to correct such molecular genetic aberrations.

The threat of bipolar disorder is even more frightening if we consider a series of facts. Bipolar disorder very likely is the most serious and frequent mental illness affecting both adults and children in our country. A good majority of people suffering from drug addiction also suffer from bipolar disorder. It is very likely that, in such people, the drug addiction may not have occurred if bipolar disorder had not predisposed them to establish such an addiction. Bipolar disorder triggers impulsive behavior which is a risk factor for contracting HIV infection and bipolar disorder is common among people affected by HIV. Many people affected by bipolar disorder commit suicide, many end up in prisons, and it is perhaps the single most important reason for family break up. A good majority of children and adolescents brought to psychiatric settings suffer from bipolar disorder. And the list goes on and on...

It is a fact these days that there are more mentally ill people in some of our jails than in the nearby psychiatric hospitals. Psychiatric hospitals are closing as part of the government cost-cutting measures the coalition of selfishness has been demanding. The majority of the mentally ill in jails suffer from bipolar disorder in one form or another. It is very likely that many people facing the death penalty (especially in states where the coalition under discussion has its sway) suffer from bipolar disorder or related mood disorders. These disorders may have gone undiagnosed or ignored out of convenience by those in authority.

No private company is going to pursue basic research that may take several decades—even centuries—to produce worthwhile results. The genetic and related abnormalities that underlie illnesses such as bipolar disorder, schizophrenia, and other neurodegenerative diseases require solutions, but they will remain unsolved, if left to for-profit companies. Private companies would rather tinker at the edges of medicines that are already available and market them as revolutionary products. And then they can take their huge profits and go on to the next money-making project. The medicines that are available today for serious psychiatric and neurological problems are very inadequate for the purpose. Also, they produce unacceptable side effects that make the majority of patients object to taking them. The pharmaceutical companies, however, market them as miraculous drugs. And the companies make their exorbitant profits by selling them at prices no one can afford.

The fact is that there has been very little progress made in the treatment of illnesses such as bipolar disorder and schizophrenia in the past forty years. Yet drug companies have come out with one miracle drug after another by making minor changes in the chemical structure of the inadequate and not-very-acceptable drugs already available. Few (if any) of these medicines have been any more effective than what has been available for almost forty years. The side effects have not been much better, though the drug companies have touted their marvelous benefits in all these areas. Of course, the claims of the drug companies have turned out to be mostly false propaganda time and again.

It is as if, the destiny of human race hinges on finding permanent solutions to these illnesses—especially mental illnesses such as bipolar disorder, schizophrenia, and viral illnesses (such as AIDS), and the various cancers that affect us, and neurological disorders such as autism, Parkinsonism, and Alzheimer's. We cannot rely on drug companies to save humanity. It is our duty, and we the people (who constitute the government) should take the lead in finding solutions to these problems. Cutting taxes for the richest in the country and drastically cutting government spending for research just won't do it—despite what the superrich led coalition claims.

If for no other reason than to find cures for the devastating maladies that destroy our minds and bodies, we need to defeat the coalition of the selfish. And we need a concerned government to take a leading role in this action. In short, we need to promote a government that is really concerned about the plight of all human beings.

Vote!

# CHAPTER VII
# A COALITION THAT REJECTS SCIENCE AND GIVES PROMINENCE TO FUNDAMENTALISM AND GREED AT ANY COST

A great deal of progress for humanity that has occurred during the recent centuries has been due to advancements in science and technology. Until a century or two back, human life expectancy was very short because most people did not have enough food, there were no effective medicines to combat common infections and infestations, no vaccines to prevent diseases, and only limited access to clean water. And those are just a few of the problems that made life on earth extremely difficult for previous generations. Thanks to our scientists, unselfish people, and concerned governments, we now have many effective medicines. Notably, we have antibiotics that can control many bacterial infections and vaccines that can prevent many of the bacterial and viral infections that killed and crippled our ancestors. These infections were a serious problem as recently as a few generations back.

Diseases such as typhoid, tuberculosis, bacterial pneumonia, syphilis, and polio could kill or cripple most of the people afflicted by them a century or so back. Today, those diseases can be cured or prevented in most cases by relatively simple measures. The vaccines we have today, the vaccines our scientists invented, have made illnesses such as polio and small pox almost nonexistent in the world. Our children can be effectively immunized against most serious and frequent childhood illnesses of the past. We have ways of protecting our food supply. We can start at the farms where food is produced and move down the line to the stores from where we buy the food and our food supply is protected. We can use scientific measures to not only increase output from our farms but also prevent the spread of food-borne illnesses. Advances in agriculture have increased the food supply all over the world to a remarkable degree. All these scientific and public health measures have made our lives so much more comfortable than what our ancestors had to endure.

There was no dearth of prayer, belief, or disciplined living on the part of our ancestors, but there was no end to their suffering. It was progress in science and scientific thinking that made life on earth more tolerable, unless one holds on to the belief that life on this earth is meant to be as miserable and short as it can be, so that, we could earn our badges of suffering and move on as quickly as possible to what many of us have the freedom to believe in – the life after in paradise. The fact is that even the most pious believer has a body and mind to take care of in this world. Nothing good comes out of suffering from miserable illnesses that destroy the body and mind. Fundamentalism would not be enough to protect us from unnecessary misery on earth, and fundamentalism that rejects science can only bring more misery to all human beings.

Elections are about making a better life for everyone on this earth (in the comprehensive sense of total well-being). Elections are less about reaching the afterlife in paradise. Moreover, there is a separation of state and religion in our constitution and way of life.

A good, democratic political system should let everyone have a chance to believe what they want to believe. As long a person's beliefs do not interfere with another's rights (and the beliefs are not unnecessarily burdensome to others), that person should be able to hold on to those beliefs. Elections and democracy, though, are more about life on earth with as little intrusion of religious beliefs into the political arena as possible.

Through the advancement of science, we have come to recognize our precariousness and defects as human beings. Everyone has the right to believe they are God's very special creations (and should be guided by the various religious beliefs as they were handed down millennia back). Still, as human beings with brains made to logically understand our circumstances (except those unfortunate ones who are limited by brain defects), we must recognize that such beliefs have their limitations if blindly followed. No matter what, we are all prone to diseases, defects, old age, and eventual death. (And events leading up to most deaths are not too pleasant, most of us will agree.) Logical and rational thinking is essential to navigate our way through our lives and reduce suffering, which is an inevitable part of human existence. We need to temper our faith and belief system with enough rationality—otherwise, we may do harm to ourselves and others without even intending to do so.

Today, there is a great deal of rhetoric often coming from those who seem to be persuaded by their history and circumstances to hold on to a closed-mindedness rooted in fundamentalism. This includes rejection of science and alignment with policies that favor the superrich. And those policies aim to dictate what others should believe. They want ordinary people to follow their beliefs, closed mindedness, and rejection of science in a manner that can only be disastrous to the world and produce misery to most human beings. Many such people have either not faced the harsh realities of life—either because they are too young or because they are too fortunate or unfortunate to be insulated from such realities of the lives of many people. This predisposes them to carry on with their eccentric pronouncements and remain pathologically closed-minded. Leaders so insulated and predisposed, can only lead anyone who follows them, into the land of ignorance, prejudice, and harm (to themselves and others).

The combination of threat of fundamentalism, rejection of science, and ideologies that favor the superrich and explains away the plight of the middle class and the poor is quite a destructive combination. This threat is a strong enough reason to vote in the coming election. We must prevent such forces from coming into power and dictating our lives.

Vote!

# CHAPTER VIII
## A THREAT TO THE HEALTH CARE REFORM LAW, MEDICARE, AND MEDICAID

For those who have not had reason to be concerned about Medicaid, Medicare, and the health care reform law enacted by the present administration, a few introductory remarks may not seem too out of place or a waste of time.

Medicaid is the government program of health care for those with very low income or no income at all. Medicare is the government program for those who are over sixty-five years old (and for those who are permanently disabled and unable to work because of that disability). Medicaid is paid for with government funds. Medicare is paid for, primarily, with the Medicare taxes every taxpayer pays (and from premiums collected from beneficiaries). A lot of people—especially young people or people under sixty-five—do not know what Medicaid or Medicare is. After all, they've never had to apply to either program. However they are of major concern if one unfortunately is, or becomes poor, or if one becomes permanently disabled, or reaches age sixty-five. So it's helpful to develop some knowledge about these programs as early as we can.

These programs (Medicaid and Medicare) cover the health care expenses of a very large segment of our population, and they cost a great deal of money. For a long time, the coalition of selfishness has been railing against these programs. They want to privatize these programs or eliminate them entirely. This would force the elderly and disabled to be at the mercy of private, for-profit companies. It would make the poor look for charity or go without any medical care. They want senior citizens to buy health insurance from for-profit, private companies—and the companies get to decide which services they will pay for and what they will not. Imagine a situation in which a feeble, bed ridden eighty- or ninety-year-old person begs to get insurance or services from one of these for-profit companies. The companies could say no to any service or decide which services they will approve and which ones they will not. They could decide to only pay for part of the amount of the person's medical bills. The poor, elderly person's preoccupation and constant worry before leaving this world is to have to argue, fight, and be rejected by these greedy, for-profit companies for one service or benefit or another or, even worse, they might have to go without any care at all.

If we have to beg, plead, and argue in those circumstances, let it be with our own government program, (set up and managed by a government we installed by election). At least when our time comes, we would know that we got a fair deal like anyone else, sharing what our country could afford to give us. After all, that is how families function: sharing what they have in a just manner. At least we would not be subjected to the humiliations of a money-grabbing insurance company that wants to penny-pinch on our death beds, so that they can have their unfair profits.

There are some things we want our government (which basically is ourselves) to be responsible for. One of them is our health care expenses when we are elderly, disabled, or extremely poor.

Interestingly, the people and insurance companies who criticize the government for providing health care programs for the citizens who need it and cannot afford the exorbitant private premiums and who insist that the government should not be involved in the health care arena at all, are already grabbing large chunks of the government programs presently in existence, through 'managed care' (private companies taking over government programs and government monies and using that money to ration out services and in the process making a profit for themselves as middlemen!).

At present, there are many, many private companies involved in this racket. A lot of the time, people who are subjected to such "managing" by these managed care companies do not even know which company is managing their lives. After all, the companies use mysterious names and subdivisions, and they change like chameleons. They transfer and manipulate care and services to their advantage with little concern for the person who is the recipient of those services. The administrative costs and frustrations caused to the recipient and time lost for everyone in the process (ever dialed one of those numbers – good luck!) could all be avoided if the private companies stay out of taking over and managing the health care rights we earned through hard work and contributions.

We have to resist the attempt by the selfish and the superrich to privatize Medicare and Medicaid. We do not want to beg and plead with the greedy, private companies that collude with the selfish coalition by giving them big donations and more. We don't want these hassles when we are poor, infirm, or in the last days of our lives on this earth (and unable to defend or argue for ourselves).

Those representing the coalition of selfishness, even the ones who once touted a health care reform with an individual mandate for their state, and now shamelessly ridicule the present health care law and want to get elected on the platform that the first day in office they will repeal the present law that gives hope to the uninsured Americans. They have no legitimate answer to the plight of fifty million uninsured Americans, and they don't care. Also, they don't want anyone to pin them down with that question. They want us to stay ignorant and unconcerned. They want us to cheer them on when they utter absolute foolishness and lack of concern for the plight of the uninsured Americans.

It is worth repeating: if we have to argue about any unfairness in health care, let it be with ourselves, our government. At least we will know what the limitations are—and that all of us have to face and accept those limitations, not because some greedy, private company wants to make a profit when we are infirm or on our death bed.

Let this be one of the top reasons to vote in 2012 and vote against the coalition of selfishness.

Vote!

# Chapter IX
## The Evolving Understanding about the Human Being—If Only Things Were So Simple

For thousands of years, mankind, faced with all the uncertainties and troubles that could come our way on this earth, tried to make some sense out of our lives on earth. The result was an evolving concept of us, humans, our nature, and whether life on earth made any sense at all or whether it was just an accidental occurrence in this mysterious and unpredictable universe. Who can blame our ancestors (or any one of us) for clutching at straws and trying to find some meaning and sustaining comfort when faced with the realities of this world: a life that starts and ends with more questions left than answered; children born deformed with little chance for a reasonable life and requiring life long care and their existence making not much sense; disparities in intelligence and physical capacities and circumstances of birth that relegate many to second-class status; illnesses that come in myriads of forms and cause havoc in life; life taken away suddenly by one calamity or another (earthquakes, tsunamis, and hurricanes that hit us time and again and make us question the sense of it all); the unjust systems of the world, mental illnesses that destroy millions upon millions of lives from having any chance in this world at all and leaving us with a life of torture from beginning to end; illnesses that are inherited that make us act bizarrely or violently, or drive us to suicide and prevent us from having any worthwhile freedom,; viruses that sneak into our bodies and destroy us in one blow (or unleash a relentless process that robs us of our strength and dignity before snuffing us out for good); degenerative illnesses that are programmed into us even before birth like time bombs; alcohol and drug addiction for which millions of us are predisposed to; these and countless other vagaries of life that do not make much sense to anyone—perhaps even to the mystics among us.

Who can blame our ancestors for coming to the conclusion that life on earth does not make sense and, it made sense only if we believed in an afterlife in which life's iniquities, miseries, and bizarreness would be explained. It would make sense if we could exist in a state of perpetual bliss with our creator, whom religions call by various names (and fight about causing more havoc).

Our religions sprung from ideas that came out of the ponderings of millions of our forefathers in near and distant lands. Our religious leaders, whom many of us venerate, have given voice to many of their conclusions from time to time. Many—if not most of us—are born into and brought up with belief systems that depend on the circumstances of our birth and upbringing. Some of us believe (or try to believe, or are required to believe) in these religious beliefs or systems to a greater or lesser degree. And all of these beliefs have the common thread that they are beyond rational understanding or explanations. Rather than look at these religious ideas or beliefs as works in progress, many of us believe (or are forced to believe) that there is nothing to be explained or understood beyond what is in the sacred texts. Many of the calamities man has brought upon himself are based on such rigid beliefs and attempts to claim one's belief system is the only true one or is superior to others. Therein lie the problem of fundamentalism and fanaticism—irrespective of what religious belief it is based upon.

Fundamentalism makes us blind—like the misguided fanatics who caused mayhem on 9/11. They believed they were doing God's work and had a straight passport to heaven earned via their evil deed. They could not crush our spirits because we could see through their closed-mindedness and fanaticism without giving into blind fundamentalism and fanaticism ourselves. It prevented us from running around in rage and acting violently toward innocent people, just because they were of some faith or persuasion different than ours. Fundamentalism makes us intolerant of others who do not share our beliefs, which is not rational to start with. Fundamentalism thrust into the political and policy-making arenas can only cause misery for the majority of people as it is an irrational system and can ruin people's lives.

Our understanding of ourselves—our biology, our brain and how it works and affects our thinking and actions, what can go wrong and produce which adverse effects, the workings of the universe, our earth itself— all these are only at a preliminary stage today. It is through progress in science that we will understand more about ourselves, our earth, and the universe and subsequently work toward making life on earth more tolerable to humans. For this, we have to devote enough money and resources to the study of science and research to make progress in these areas … from generation to generation. At the same time we have to stay rational, committed to democracy and peace, and tolerant of other ideas and beliefs—no matter how bizarre they may appear, as long as they do not infringe on the rights of others or endanger them. Such explorations and the incorporation of new understandings in science and the democratic process into policy making for the benefit of all is essential for the welfare and progress of humanity. To deny such activities, which the alliance of selfishness has insisted on, invites disaster. Such denial will only make the plight of humans more miserable and the progress toward a better life on earth for all people an impossible task.

We need to oppose people who resist such progress for humanity. It is another reason to vote in the 2012 election and advance the cause of human progress.

Vote!

# CHAPTER X
# DNA

The DNA (deoxyribonucleic acid) we were given by God, the big bang, or both, or accidentally and how we are made as biological beings, influence or dictate our lives as humans to a great degree and are relevant to issues we face in the coming election.

It is only in the past fifty years or so we started getting a better idea of what substance humans are made of and how it influences the way we think, feel, and act. We've started to understand how DNA controls our bodies function and what illnesses of the body and mind we may be more or less susceptible to because of problems in the DNA each individual inherits.

For those who are not very familiar with the topic of DNA and cell biology, the DNA in our cells is the crucial component that makes us what we are. It is not too much of an exaggeration to say that DNA is destiny for most people. It is the DNA that determines, more than anything else, how we look, whether we are predisposed to a reasonably healthy life physically and mentally, and how susceptible or not we may be to various illnesses that plague mankind and myriads of our positive and negative characteristics. It even plays a crucial role in determining what our temperament and personality might be. It is a sobering thought that many of our great thinkers who lived in the past centuries— including religious leaders who we worship—had little idea what DNA was. They did not know how crucial it was in determining a great deal of the fate of a human being.

This does not mean DNA determines everything about our lives. It only means, given average circumstances— whatever that may be, it will determine our chances or capacity for reasonable accomplishments in life. It will also determine our probability of reasonable health (including mental health and having a reasonable personality that others find not too difficult to deal with). This does not mean DNA determines everything. You can have the best DNA traits in the world, but if you are born into an environment that is fanatical or stifling, or blinding you of the capacity to be open minded, your DNA may not save you. The environmental components—by this, I mean not just the physical environment, but also the cultural, religious, and historical aspects—might prove to be too destructive to give rise to a reasonable human being. The environment may even destroy you, as it has done to some great thinkers and leaders throughout human history who happened to get caught in such environments or cultural contexts. But given a reasonable, health-promoting environment, inheriting positive traits through one's DNA places a person at a distinct advantage over someone less endowed.

I bring this point up in the present context to open the discussion that what we have known and decided about us, the human beings, through the last two millennia or more, has to undergo a revolutionary transformation in view of what we are just beginning to understand about ourselves in view of the role DNA plays in producing the uniqueness of each individual. It is very likely that a great deal of judgments humans made about themselves and others throughout human history may be highly questionable, if we look at the understandings that are developing about DNA and related molecular biological mechanisms. In view of this and related emerging knowledge, it is essential that we develop an open-minded and rational approach to understanding ourselves and our fellow beings and their strengths and defects, especially when making judgments on what we consider to be deviations or defects in others.

A cautious, non-dogmatic, and open-minded approach in all matters pertaining to our fellow human beings, the world at large, and even our worst adversaries is essential. Otherwise, we run the risk of judging others and taking condemning actions that are plainly wrong. One day, the future generations will be astonished by how ignorant and foolish we were—especially in terms of the judgments we made about others and even condemning others to death.

The coalition of the unscientific and the closed-minded wants us to keep believing nothing but what was written and proclaimed millennia back. But back then man had little idea what science was or what material we were made of and how it influenced almost everything about us, including our personality, our proneness to mental and physical illnesses, our sexual orientation, and our capacity to even make a living. Once we are enlightened about these and related issues, we will become less judgmental when dealing with others and accept that we are all in it together—the human predicament.

In order to accomplish this, we need to have a government that will promote further explorations in this area and incorporate such understandings into public policy for the benefit of all. The coalition of closed-mindedness will thwart any such explorations and progress.

Vote!

# CHAPTER XI
## PREJUDICE, PERSECUTION, AND SEXUAL ORIENTATION

There is little doubt that people with sexual orientations different from that of people who have an exclusively heterosexual orientation, existed as a hidden (or not-so-hidden) minority in all cultures from time immemorial. These are people whose sexual orientation is homosexual or bisexual. It also includes those whose gender identity places them in a misunderstood—and often persecuted— minority. Arguably, no other minority group in the world has experienced as much prejudice, discrimination, and fear about their true, nature-given feelings and how much control or not they had over such feelings and instincts as those of people with non-heterosexual orientation.

Though, in the past few decades, considerable progress has been made to thwart overt prejudice and discrimination against people with such orientations and identities, much work needs to be done. There is little doubt that life for people who belong to such minorities continues to be a much harder journey than for others. Misunderstandings, misinformation, millennia-old prejudices, and fears still persist. Our religious dogmas and interpretations about homosexuality have added to the misinformation, prejudice, and outright hostility aimed at such people. People who are religious fundamentalists and those who are closed minded, especially closed-minded about scientific facts and what explorations in study of society and culture inform us, continue to want to believe that homosexuality is a choice that bad people willfully make. They refuse to consider scientific evidence that such orientations are a distinct aspect of human nature that is rooted in human biology. They fail to acknowledge that, just as people given a heterosexual orientation do not choose to be heterosexual but, are instinctively programmed for such orientation, those given a homosexual orientation by nature have no choice in the matter and that it is as instinctive and rooted in human biology and very likely programmed by variations in human DNA and prenatal through childhood brain development.

Anyone who has had enough exposure to the field of human development and studying human nature and mental health issues cannot but be impressed by the fact that such orientations are variations that occur in nature and people themselves have nothing to do with their given orientations. Whether there are some subtle environmental contributions that tip the scale in one direction or another has been discussed for some time, but neither the evidence for this is strong, nor is there any evidence that trying to change a person's sexual orientation is beneficial or successful in any manner. What evidence there is, points to the possibility of bad consequences, especially if a dogmatic approach is taken in the matter.

In simple terms, all evidence indicates that homosexuality is a natural variation that occurs in a significant percent of human beings. It may be difficult for many people to accept this fact, but we can remind ourselves that there are many given variations in nature and humans are no exception. There are facts about us, humans – often, even bewildering and painful ones, that vary from the good-old fairy tales that, all people can decide to be just good or bad, a genius or unintelligent, heterosexual or homosexual, if only they tried or had well-meaning parents, or read the right books and believed in them one-hundred percent and so on.

Let us not forget that it is heterosexual (or mostly heterosexual) parents that bring homosexual children into this world. Let us at least strive for an open mind and acceptance so that the lives of people with a homosexual orientation will not be as difficult as it has been through history and the difficulties people with such orientations face will disappear as soon as possible. This change requires an open mind, an acceptance of scientific facts, and an attitude of tolerance toward people who are different in nature than those who may be in the majority.

Discrimination toward people with a homosexual orientation has not lessened because for-profit, private companies and fundamentalist groups have taken the initiative in that matter. It is a good reminder for us that the claim that the government should only be involved in the defense of the country and, private enterprise will solve all other issues, is just that – a fantasy. It is the activism of people who knew what such misunderstanding and discrimination was doing to them—as well as responsive and enlightened governments—that accomplished the progress that has been made in this area. And we have miles to go yet!

Protecting the freedoms of such minorities and ending discrimination against them, is another reason to vote against the coalition of the fundamentalists and the closed-minded, backed by and spear headed by the money of the super-rich.

Vote!

# CHAPTER XII
## POOR—A DIRTY WORD
## IN THIS ELECTION

Imagine a candidate running for the highest office in the nation uttering these words: "I am not concerned about the very poor," and then quickly scrambling to mouth the words advisors whisper in his ear to "flip-flop" to gain votes. (Anyone remember the candidate in question?)

Imagine, if a person running for president of the United States spontaneously said that he or she was not concerned about the very poor. What kind of person is it whose soul harbors such callous attitude that, it spontaneously comes out of his mouth (even when he is meticulously managed by his handlers to conceal his true feelings and beliefs and choose his words carefully to win the election). It is beyond the good old "Freudian slip". Think also, what kind of person harbors such deep-seated prejudice and apathy toward the poorest among us and then flip-flops and end up mouthing the words his or her handlers dictate, to make him come across as a concerned person - all for the purpose of attaining power. Fortunately for us, in the process, we got to see what kind of callous attitude the person really harbors—and where his priorities lie.

It takes a lifetime of disconnect from the problems of the poor to utter such words. The explanation the poor have a safety net is also hollow. The fact is that whatever safety net poor people have had in the past decades is being shred to pieces by the alliance led by the superrich. The coalition of selfishness has come to the understanding that if the services and expenses for the poor (and those teetering on the edge of poverty) are cut, all will be well with America and the wallets of the well-to-do.

Those who utter callous phrases—such as, "I am not concerned about the very poor"—harbor exactly such ideas and feelings within themselves. Despite their effort and guidance from their handlers, these ideas bubble up and come to the surface because their souls are full of such beliefs and prejudices. You don't have to be a Freudian scholar to figure that out. Even after being coached to cover up their true feelings, the more they explain, the more it becomes clear where their true feelings lie. As they fumble and bumble for words as to what they should have said, and the more they try to explain to redeem themselves, the more it becomes evident that their explanations lack substance and conviction. What comes out of a person's mouth spontaneously reflects a person's true feelings – more often than not.

A look at the past lives of such people reveal where their priorities were. How they spent the best part of their lives and how much effort they put into helping the poor and disadvantaged (compared to the time and effort they put into amassing money and power and catering to the rich) is telling. It is a path of pursuit of affluence followed by pursuit of power that they have followed in their lives. They never gave themselves a chance to immerse themselves in the problems of the poor during their formative years. Thus they never developed the capacity to empathize with the problems of the poor. They are not concerned (and are very satisfied) if the poor get caught in the "safety net" for ever, like fish caught in a fishing-net and writhing to get out, but can't.

*Poor* has become a dirty word in this election. It is as if spending money for the poor, the disabled, and the disadvantaged is the reason for all our troubles. It is as if anyone who mentions concern for such groups will be vilified—their words and concerns distorted, and they will be branded socialists, liberals, or worse ... and run out of town.

If we allow those who have no compassion, no understanding, and no empathy for the poor, the disabled, and the medically disenfranchised to come into power, their ideology and true feelings will rule the day. And the plight of the poor will become worse.

Yes, we do have a responsibility for those who have very little and let not the selfish coalition make "poor" a dirty and feared word in this election.

Vote!

# CHAPTER XIII
# HEALTH INSURANCE FOR ALL—A
# CAUSE WORTH FIGHTING FOR

Providing an opportunity to get health insurance for the millions—about fifty million at the last count—who do not have it has become a vilified cause. Is there any rationale behind such vilification, other than pure selfishness on the part of some who have it and others who are selfish and do not want any resources spent on the less fortunate? The answer is a resounding no!

If Canada can give all its citizens affordable health insurance, why can't the United States? Those who criticize the Canadian system and scare Americans with misinformation do not have much of an idea what they are talking about. Anyone who has firsthand experience of the Canadian and American systems would refrain from such senseless talk. It is probably true that some doctors and others who want to make a lot of money (and some people who are very wealthy and can afford anything) probably would prefer the cumbersome and prejudiced system that we have in our country today. But the fifty million Americans who do not have any insurance—and those who understand and sympathize with their plight—would not claim we have a wonderful system. These disadvantaged citizens would not want to keep the system as it is.

Any country worth its name should be able to provide affordable medical care to its citizens. The only way, in today's world, that such medical services can be made accessible to all people is through affordable medical insurance. And the only way all citizens can have affordable medical insurance is to require that all people have insurance (and make it affordable for everyone), whether they are employed or unemployed. Because the economy has gone through a recession (set forth by mismanagement by the last administration), the number of unemployed still remains high. Many are unemployed, underemployed, or do not make enough money to purchase adequate medical insurance on their own. The prices quoted by private companies for purchase of adequate medical insurance for an individual or a family is shockingly high. Those without insurance are afraid to go see doctors or approach hospitals or clinics for medical care. They fear the frightening expenses, the unknowns regarding the bills they will be slapped with, or just being afraid and embarrassed to reveal they have no medical insurance.

The coalition of the superrich and selfish has unleashed a brainwashing propaganda that, providing medical insurance for all citizens is socialism and hence, should not even be a consideration for Americans.   According to them, making it possible for all citizens to buy affordable medical insurance and requiring that all people carry insurance will somehow make the United States a totalitarian regime and it will destroy our constitutional right to liberty and the pursuit of happiness. Some—even in our esteemed Supreme Court—seem to think that a person who considers himself or herself healthy does not have to have insurance, and God forbid they are suddenly afflicted by a catastrophic illness, they can just pick up the phone and get whatever coverage they want without any trouble and all will be well. It is a pity how out of touch some people are. There are those who are privileged enough to have health insurance all their lives—often because they work a government job or work in a large enough private organization that provides coverage. Just like the lucky congressman and senators, even those who will work tirelessly to deny health insurance for the fifty-million Americans who do not have it—let us not forget them!

Impressive—though not fully satisfactory—have been the strides the present administration has made in making affordable health insurance for the citizens a reality in the coming years. However, by using derogatory-sounding names, the privileged and selfish try to confuse ordinary people. They try to make ordinary people think that giving everyone a chance to have affordable health insurance is a terrible idea. They say that anyone who supports such an idea is a Socialist or a Communist and should be punished. They brainwash us with such propaganda. They don't want us to think about the plight of fifty million Americans who do not have any health insurance. What good is a country if it cannot make health insurance a right for its citizens? If we call ourselves a country, we should implement measures that will make accessible and affordable medical care and insurance a right for all citizens. We should pool our resources together to make sure that none of our fellow citizens suffer the indignity of being afraid (because of financial reasons) to see a doctor or go to an emergency room.

Our neighbors to the north, Canadians, put us to shame by providing universal health insurance for all their citizens. No Canadian thinks twice when he or she has to see a doctor, go to an emergency room, be hospitalized, have surgery, seek psychiatric help, or attend to any health-related need. But many of us Americans shudder at such a thought. We are too embarrassed and frightened to answer questions about not having health insurance (or adequate insurance), or having to pay exorbitant amounts as a co-pay, or being told something will not be covered, or having to leave the hospital with our surgical wounds still bleeding, our mental health needs not met, or worst of all, not knowing what to do when our children are ill.

The unconcerned leaders of the coalition for the superrich and the selfish are shouting at the top of their voice how everyone should look after themselves and the government has no right or reason to make affordable health care accessible to all citizens. We should wonder what reality they are talking about. Who are they talking about? Do they have any concern for the fifty million American citizens who do not have any health insurance? When they gloat that they will repeal the present health care law the first day they are in office (and the closed-minded followers clap and shout as if it were the greatest achievement they could think of), we should wonder what reality they live in, what planet they're from.

It is time to oppose this brainwashing that we have been subjected to and work toward advancing the cause of affordable health insurance as a fundamental right of all citizens. The only way we can accomplish this task is by voting against the coalition of the superrich, the selfish, and the closed-minded. By voting against them, we can free ourselves and our fellow citizens from the perpetual fear and anxiety caused by not having health insurance.

Remember what members of this coalition have promised if they come into power: they will reverse all the progress the present administration has achieved in the area of affordable health care and insurance. They will take us back to square one with no hope of having any such thing in our lifetime. We have been trying for health insurance for all for many generations, and if the coalition of the selfish takes it away from us, we may be doomed. Remember the excitement and applause in their forums when their candidates were making statements that, if a person who does not have health insurance is dying in an intensive care unit because of lack of insurance and money to pay for the expenses, it should not be any concern of ours, because everyone is responsible for themselves, and if you are in bad luck in this world you should just accept your plight and say goodbye to the world when others go about their merry way. No, that is not the American way. Let us vote against this misguided and unconcerned coalition that brainwashes us into believing that we should not be concerned about our fellow citizens.

The affordable health care reform act that the present administration managed to put in place (though far from perfect) is a lifesaver for our country. It relieves our fellow citizens and ourselves from perpetual anxiety and uncertainty regarding our health care needs. Do not let this coalition take it away as it has vowed to do if it attains power.

Yes, our votes do matter. Vote against this coalition of selfishness so that we and all our brothers, sisters, children, parents, friends, neighbors—all citizens of this great country—will be assured affordable medical insurance and care throughout our lives – from birth to death, as a right of citizenship. Let us get that one worry out of our lives. This is our chance before the selfish coalition snatches it away from us.

Yes, this is our chance. Let us act decisively!

Vote!

I write this knowing the Supreme Court could throw more complexities our way before the 2012 elections. If we have the will we'll have the way to overcome whatever obstacles are thrown our way! We will not rest until all Americans have a chance to get affordable health insurance. Justice is on our side!

# CHAPTER XIV
# THE MYTH THAT ALL
# CHILDREN ARE BORN WITH
# EQUAL CAPACITIES

The pronouncements of some of the leaders of the coalition of selfishness have tried to perpetuate the myth that all children are born with equal capacities. They say that if families followed the ideology of the fundamentalists and superrich, everyone would grow up to be highly capable and disciplined adults. Everyone would be thoroughly capable of mastering even the most difficult subjects—and everyone would become affluent or superrich as they are. We would therefore have no unemployment problem. After all, companies are starving for highly capable scientists and technologists. They argue that the problem is just that the children of the poor are lazy—and they have learned laziness from the people around them who do not work. (Remember the idea put forward by a coalition leader that the children clean the toilets in school to learn work ethic because the adults they live with are lazy and do not work)

Anyone who has been a parent and has an open mind, any teacher who has struggled with the educational issues of children, anyone who has tried to study the intellectual and emotional capacities and problems of children, all know that children are born with unequal capacities not only in the intellectual and physical spheres, but more importantly, in their emotional capacities and stability as well. The fact is, without inherent emotional stability, no one can effectively use any other capacities well (or consistently). Such capacities are necessary to succeed in the world, whether it is in education, employment, family, social life, or some other area.

To believe—based on misinformation—that all children can master and excel in all subjects if they make the effort is also a myth. Many children, due to the inherent capacities of their brains, can do very well with minimal or average effort in subjects such as mathematics. Other children (those lacking such capacities) struggle to achieve even the minimum standards in spite of a great deal of effort. We are all familiar with children who struggle to achieve proficiency in reading and writing in spite of their efforts. There are significant, inherent variations in these capacities. Blaming the children and their parents for not making everyone high-performing scientists and technologists is unfair. After telling children for decades that they can study whatever they want to and everything will be all right, we now blame them for not being little Einsteins. Interestingly, many politicians who blame the children and their parents never bothered to pursue the paths they are now blaming the young people for not pursuing.

We, as a society, have to prepare to accommodate the varying capacities, strengths, and weaknesses of children we bring into this world. To believe that all children have same capacities and if any child is unable to make it successfully in this highly competitive world, it is the child's laziness and lack of discipline, which in turn is caused by their parents' attitude, is worse than saying that all overweight people are overweight because they lack discipline and are lazy. The fact is, there are hundreds of thousands of children born every year who are destined to face a difficult life, just based on their biological capacities alone. It is clear many will struggle. By this, I don't mean only children who are born with severe deformities or intellectual deficiencies that knock them out of reasonable chances to succeed in this world from day one and leave their parents with heart breaks they may never overcome.

Enormous as these problems are, more enormous is the problem of children who appear to have it all when they are born, but as in the case of a flower that unfolds from a bud, in many instances starts showing defects of one petal or another that mars its perfection for known or unknown reasons, so also, as many of these children born to any of us can spontaneously start exhibiting weaknesses in their capacities, both in specific areas of academics, or more importantly, in emotional and behavioral realms. In the majority of these situations, these interferences and defects are due to biological mechanisms—mostly DNA imperfections—that manifest their defects in subtle and not-so-subtle ways. And these defects are often bad enough to ruin lives. I am not discounting the extremely important—perhaps *all-important*—role parents play in the development and well-being of children. Still, in many cases, the subtle and poorly understood biological factors based on our genetic inheritance trump all the efforts parents can put in to help a child.

Perhaps in the distant future mankind will find some solution to such genetic and brain development imperfections. Until then, we must discard the myth that all children are created equal. Left to the coalition we are talking about nothing but blaming the parents and the children will continue.

As parents who are unfortunate to have such children (they may even be a majority in our country soon) and all people dedicated to the wellbeing of children suffering from severe learning or emotional problems and have struggled to understand and rectify their problems know, these problems are too complex and even mysterious to be just blamed on the lack of dedication on the part of parents.

There may be millions of children growing up in America today who fall into this category. Millions of children who, in spite of their efforts and their parents' efforts, may not get a decent chance at life that many others take for granted. Many will not be able to master the kinds of subjects today's highly complex and competitive world rewards with adequately paying jobs. And there is another greater tragedy: the emotionally impaired group, of which, many, may not even get a chance to live a very ordinary life or enjoy any freedom. This tragedy of human nature, as it stands today, significantly affects our country—perhaps more so than many other places in the world. It cannot be dismissed by ignorant statements and an unwillingness to understand and face the complex and unpleasant reality.

Many in the political coalition under discussion here have no time or desire to accept and understand such complexities. Rather, they are committed to spreading their beliefs that categorize humanity into two groups: the lazy and the hardworking, the disciplined and the undisciplined, the true believers and the heathens. Nothing could be further from the truth.

They would like to believe (and they want us to believe) that all the problems of mankind would be solved if we read and reread books written millennia back and practice the logical and illogical in them blindly.

A great deal of the problems of the types of children mentioned above, especially those children who are emotionally unstable, and subsequently out of control with their behavior which denies them from having a fair chance in life, result in their ending up as dysfunctional adults. Most of these aberrations, on careful scrutiny, is heavily or entirely propelled by biological factors they inherit. More often than not, if there is laziness or bad examples set by their parents, as the coalition ridicules, on closer scrutiny, such parents' problems may also, to varying degrees, be manifestations of such biological vulnerabilities, in many, if not in most cases. Many people may have difficulty believing this, as they may not have had the opportunity to study such issues in depth and with an open mind.

Blaming parents, cutting aid, and telling the government to stay out of education and health care is just a combination of ignorance, uncaring attitude, and nothing more.

These problems with which an increasing number of our children are coming into the world today, have a tremendous impact on almost all aspects of our country, ranging from economy, unemployment, law enforcement, health care, and in general all aspects of society. We need to strengthen our social safety net. Without it, these children will have a horrendous life (which is what happens in countries without such support and we'll have a worse deal). The educational system, the health care system, the health insurance problem and who will get what type of health insurance or no insurance at all; should government be involved in any of these matters or will private companies and private insurance take care of the plights of all such unfortunate citizens are issues we need to grapple with.

The complexity, seriousness, and urgency of these matters cannot be left to the uninformed, uncaring, and prejudiced attitude of the coalition.

# Vote!

# Chapter XV
# Our Common Humanity,
# Our Common DNA, and
# Our Common Destiny

There are serious issues humanity faces as a result of defects in the biological material we are made of—specifically, the DNA we inherited from time immemorial. We Americans are not free of such problems. In fact, we may be more vulnerable than people of many other countries. These vulnerabilities include potential mental and emotional problems that sometimes begin in childhood and continue throughout our lives. The problems deny us the opportunity to have a reasonable life. Why we may be more susceptible to such problems is debatable, but it is clear that they exist and cause a great deal of suffering for individuals, families, and society itself.

The proportion of children born with afflictions of the mind caused by defects in DNA are increasing at an alarming rate. And these same problems make many vulnerable to drug addiction and other attendant problems, including the tendency to engage in high-risk behaviors, proneness to drug addiction, and HIV infection to name a few. People who have worked for a long time with serious intentions in these fields cannot escape being impressed by these facts. These problems, primarily based on genetic vulnerabilities, threaten to disrupt the very fabric of our society and our existence as a healthy nation. Very likely, the survival of our society itself depends upon finding solutions to such problems.

Unfortunately, in a fast-paced society where chasing more and more money is the main pursuit of many people, such serious matters receive little attention. The fact that Congress is deadlocked and the coalition refuses to acknowledge scientific facts and sound philosophies makes matters worse. The result is that such problems affecting the health of mind and body and determining the health and wellbeing of our nation itself are not recognized to the degree they should be. Little effort is made to remedy these all-important problems with the urgency they require.

Some of the factors affecting progress in these areas have been touched upon already in this book. These factors include the lack of interest private enterprises (set up to make profit) have in such matters and the enormity and complexity of these problems. Problems of this magnitude (on which the whole well-being of our country and even the world itself depends) can only be tackled by government or governments acting together and taking the lead in the matter. All of humanity has a stake in such a collaborative effort because genetic problems are universal. They have their roots in the origin of human genetic material itself, which probably goes back millions of years. Such efforts are more worthwhile and more urgent than efforts to colonize the moon, which some in the coalition have suggested should be a priority.

First, we need to start cleaning up the defects in the genetic material that cause so much consternation and threaten the well-being of humanity before flying off to the moon and other distant planets to colonize them. After all, if we don't resolve this issue, we'll just be carrying all our defects and problems and perpetuating misery elsewhere. We need a government truly committed to the welfare of its citizens in such all-important matters. We don't need people worrying about how much financial profit they can make from such efforts.

Tasks such as this—so enormous and so urgent—can only be tackled by commitment and allocation of resources by a president and legislature who understand the importance of such matters. It will never come from the coalition of the superrich, the fundamentalists, who reject science and the closed-minded. This is a very important reason to vote against such a coalition in 2012. It cannot be over-stated.

Vote!

# CHAPTER XVI
## ATTACKING A WOMAN'S RIGHT TO LIVE A REASONABLE LIFE

Recently, in preparation for the 2012 election, the coalition of fundamentalists and closed-minded people spearheaded an attack on women's rights, especially with regard to the use of contraceptives and control of fertility. The superrich have joined in to exploit the situation for electoral success. Many men (who cannot claim any expertise in regard to women's concerns about birth control and fertility) feel compelled to control women's access to contraceptives and control of their fertility. The coalition we have been talking about uses this opportunity to turn the whole question into a religious freedom issue. It portrays those who support the rights of women as interfering in the practice of religion.

No rational and peace-loving person would be against another's right to believe and practice any religion. Human history has shown us that most human beings find it hard to just accept that all the difficulties that are an inevitable part of human existence and culminating in death make sense in itself. This resulted in a human quest (throughout thousands of years) to find and hold on to some belief system or other that seems to make at least partial sense of our human predicament and give life a meaning beyond what could be understood by logical thinking and our limited brain. This quest to find meaning for life—beyond the purely rational and observable—has led to religious beliefs and religions.

Religious beliefs originated mostly before scientific advances in understanding the nature of man occurred. Hence, religious beliefs are often antithetical to scientific understanding. Also, religious mores have often excessively controlled the way human beings live, especially women. With women achieving greater freedom and equality, there has been friction and tension between a woman's right to control her body and the religious world. This is especially true with regard to fertility in the modern world. This has produced friction between some religious authorities and women in general. The coalition of the fundamentalists and the closed-minded are trying to take advantage of this friction for their own political gains. They are trying to paint the conflict as one of religious freedom rather than an intrusion into the rights of a woman to be in charge of her body. Some vying for political power, such as the superrich leaders of the coalition of selfishness, are trying to muddy the waters, confuse the people, and portray themselves as protectors of religious rights. A close look at their past will often reveal that, few of them had any such convictions in the past. They will change their position just so they can attain power.

We need to resist this sinister attempt to trample on women's freedoms and portray the intrusion into women's rights as a freedom of religion issue (for purely political gains). Vote!

# Chapter XVII
# The Problem with the
# Philosophy of the Superrich

Most of us want to be rich (and some may crave to be superrich), whatever the definition of being rich or super-rich may mean to each one of us. Whether or not it's a good thing, some of us are rich or superrich by most standards. The majority of us are only getting by, and a good portion of us are just poor by any standard.

Most of us never have any personal contact with the superrich because they usually live on an entirely different planet—unless they decide to run for some high-level political office after they are tired of making all that money (or money keeps coming in and they don't know what else to do). Being superrich produces some philosophical problems in many of those lucky or smart ones whose money-making talents and dedication to money may make many of us envy them. The problem is, after one becomes very rich or superrich, one does not have much of a choice but to safeguard one's wealth. Just as not having money can keep one awake, having too much money can also keep one awake—though for different reasons.

Once you have a lot of money, whatever your philosophy was prior to having that money will very likely change. On the other hand, if you were born into money from the get-go, you probably would have grown up with the dominant philosophy of the rich: the most important thing in life is to make a lot of money and protect it. This philosophy easily translates into a certain type of selfishness and the need to justify the singular pursuit of money—and there's not much time left to worry about those who have much less. No wonder one may not be able to hold back one's true feelings: "I don't worry about the very poor," since that person has had much less chance to be truly exposed to the plight of those who are poor. The philosophy that surrounds such people during their formative years are ideas such as the following: the poor and the sick (who can't fend for themselves) should not be the concern of others; the poor and sick should not be a significant concern for the government either; and there were good old days when charitable organizations and churches took care of the sick and poor—we should just let those good old days come back again.

Two millennia back, a spiritual leader commented on how difficult it would be for a rich man to enter a certain desired state of nonmaterial tranquility. Perhaps he had special insight into what being very wealthy could do to one's outlook in life. Having spent the best part of his or her life pursuing money with a singular devotion (including, for many, focusing educational pursuits exclusively on money-making subjects) - of course, one can put in mandatory hours at some soup kitchen or spend some time in a poor country to build up a résumé, in hope it opens the door to a coveted institution of higher learning, and then having nothing to do with such poorer settings after one hits ones true pursuit of the almighty dollar), denies one the opportunity to be truly exposed to the realities of the world: issues related to poverty, concerns for those less fortunate, a true understanding of the roots of poverty (starting with the biological endowment of a person) - physically, intellectually, and emotionally, an understanding of the circumstances that surround different lives, of ones birth, advantages and disadvantages related to race, and related contributory causes.

Having all that money, now, one is caught in the fear one may lose it (and with it the privileges associated with being superrich). There is also the nagging concern—perhaps even guilt that one has spent the best part of one's life pursuing money and privilege only and the world either does not care - or most people, other than those who track the richest in glossy magazines do not know who you are— and even they may not think highly of you.

In such a context, supporting the politicians and others who will protect the interests of superrich people like oneself becomes a burning preoccupation. Some jump into politics, thinking they can attain political power and safeguard their money and interests and those of people like oneself. Some may stay focused on making money but decide to spend enormous amounts to support those who will safeguard their wealth and privileges. In this context, the Super PACs have become a great avenue for the superrich to contribute to the political candidacy of those who will safeguard their interests.

There may be exceptions to the typical fate of the superrich, but commonly, excessive amounts of money is more likely to trap one into a path akin to the one described above.

It would have been all right if they just safeguarded their money and privileges. The problem is that they see money going to those who are poor and less fortunate than they are as a threat to their way of life, not only because they may be forced to pay their fair share of taxes but, the whole philosophy of a government dedicated to ameliorating the plight of the poor as a priority is unacceptable and threatening to them. They would rather have a government that adheres to the philosophy that, if the rich are doing better and better, all will be well with the country.

Therein lies the problem of the superrich:. From the above point of view, which is inevitable for most of the very wealthy, they will only favor policies that primarily protect their money, excessive money-making opportunities, and unique privileges. Unfortunately, such policies disproportionately affect the well-being of those who have much less because they, the superrich, will force the government to spend less money on the less privileged (and on the causes that benefit the majority of the country). They become afraid that some of the money spent on such worthy causes will have to come from fair taxes on all, including them. Prosperity for all people means their share will inevitably shrink. Hence, they oppose paying their fair share of taxes and supporting programs that help those who have less.

The superrich, being smaller in number, cannot win democratic elections or influence elections significantly in a fair manner. Hence, they try to influence other groups that oppose the open-minded, ordinary people (such as the fundamentalists and those who maintain a closed-minded and conservative approach). This closed-minded group includes some in the middle class who view the unemployed and the poor as a threat to some of what they have. These people especially fear providing health insurance for those who have none—an issue of great concern and conflict recently and that will likely influence the 2012 elections.

The superrich provide money and resources, especially through the Super PACs. They essentially dictate the direction the coalition of the selfish will move to win the election (which will allow them to attain or maintain power and set policies that favor them).

These facts will remain central themes and determining factors in the coming election and beyond. They will pose great challenges to those striving for progress for the ordinary person.

For the good of the country—especially for the ordinary people, open-minded, and poor people—there is a great need to defeat the philosophy and methods advanced by the superrich and their coalition of selfishness (led and financed by Super PACs).

Vote!